J
595.6
LUN

W9-BRB-529

No Backbone!
The World of Invertebrates

Leggy Centipedes

by Natalie Lunis

Consultant: Brian V. Brown
Curator, Entomology Section
Natural History Museum of Los Angeles County

BEARPORT
PUBLISHING

NEW YORK, NEW YORK

CALUMET CITY PUBLIC LIBRARY

Credits

Cover, © John Bell and © Art Wolf; TOC, © Steve Hopkin/Ardea; 4–5, © Matthew D. Thom; 6T, © Lynette Schimming; 6M, © Frank Greenaway/Dorling Kindersley/Getty Images; 6B, © Donald Specker/Animals Animals Enterprises/Photolibrary; 7, © Kim Taylor/npl/ Minden Pictures; 8–9, © Charles Schurch Lewallen; 10T, © A.N.T. Photo Library/NHPA; 10M, © Brian Kennedy; 10B, © Tom Vezo; 11, © Robert & Linda Mitchell; 12, © Thomas Shahan; 13, © Tom Vezo/Nature Picture Library; 14, © BIOS Huguet Pierre; 15, © Tom McHugh/Photo Researchers Inc./Photolibrary; 16T, © Tom Vezo/Nature Picture Library; 16M, © Barry Mansell/Nature Picture Library; 16B, © Martin Dohrn/Nature Picture Library; 17, © Gary Meszaros/Visuals Unlimited, Inc.; 18, © Bill Beatty; 19, © Carol Hughes/Bruce Coleman Inc.; 20, © Jane Burton/Bruce Coleman Inc.; 21, © John Bell/Bruce Coleman Inc.; 22TL, © Juniors Bildarchiv/ Alamy; 22TR, © Premaphotos/Nature Picture Library; 22BL, © Yosei Minagoshi/Nature Production/Minden Pictures; 22BR, © Stephen Luk; 22Spot, © Joseph Calev/Shutterstock; 23TL, © Tom Vezo/Nature Picture Library; 23TR, © Jim Wehtje/Photodisc/Getty Images; 23BL, © John Bell/Shutterstock; 23BR, © Thomas Shahan.

Publisher: Kenn Goin
Editorial Director: Adam Siegel
Creative Director: Spencer Brinker
Original Design: Dawn Beard Creative
Photo Researcher: Q2A Media: Poulomi Basu

Library of Congress Cataloging-in-Publication Data

Lunis, Natalie.
 Leggy centipedes / by Natalie Lunis ; consultant, Brian V. Brown.
   p. cm. — (No backbone! The world of invertebrates)
 Includes bibliographical references and index.
 ISBN-13: 978-1-59716-752-9 (library binding).
 ISBN-10: 1-59716-752-5 (library binding).
 1. Centipedes—Juvenile literature. I. Title.
 QL449.5.L86 2009.
 595.6'2—dc22.
                    2008038692

Copyright © 2009 Bearport Publishing Company, Inc. All rights reserved. No part of this publication may be reproduced in whole or in part, stored in any retrieval system, or transmitted in any form or by any means, electronic, mechanical, photocopying, recording, or otherwise, without written permission from the publisher.

For more information, write to Bearport Publishing Company, Inc., 101 Fifth Avenue, Suite 6R, New York, New York 10003. Printed in the United States of America.

10 9 8 7 6 5 4 3 2 1

Contents

Long and Leggy

Centipedes are small animals with long, thin bodies.

Their name means "100 legs."

People gave them this name because centipedes look like they have that many legs.

No centipede has exactly 100 legs, however.

Some have fewer legs—and some have even more!

Most centipedes are brown, but some are brightly colored.

How Many Legs?

There are about 3,000 kinds of centipedes.

The different kinds have different numbers of legs.

Some centipedes have as few as 15 pairs of legs.

Other have more than 200 pairs.

house centipede
(15 pairs of legs)

tiger centipede
(21 pairs of legs)

A centipede with
15 pairs of legs has
a total of 30 legs.

soil centipede
(38 pairs of legs)

stone centipede
(15 pairs of legs)

Parts of the Body

A centipede's body has two main parts—a head and a **trunk**.

The head has two large **antennas** attached.

The centipede uses them for feeling and smelling.

The trunk is made up of many small parts called **segments**.

Each segment has a pair of legs attached.

trunk

legs

antennas

head

segments

A centipede's body also has a hard covering called an exoskeleton. The exoskeleton protects the centipede's soft insides.

A World of Centipedes

Centipedes live in most parts of the world.

Some live in places that have cold winters.

Others live in places that are warm all year long.

The largest kinds, such as the Peruvian giant centipede, live in hot, rainy forests.

They can be up to 12 inches (30 cm) long.

Most centipedes are less than one inch (2.5 cm) long.

Peruvian giant centipede

Day and Night

Centipedes need to spend their days in damp, shady places, or else their bodies will dry out.

They hide under leaves, between rocks, and in tree bark.

At night the air around them becomes cooler and less dry.

That's when the long, leggy creatures come out to hunt for food.

Some kinds of centipedes live in hot, dry deserts. Like all other kinds, they survive by hiding from the sun and heat during the day and coming out only at night.

giant desert centipede

CALUMET CITY PUBLIC LIBRARY

Catching a Meal

The first two legs on a centipede's body are different from the rest.

Each one is really a poison claw.

The centipede uses the claws to catch and kill the small animals that it eats.

First it grabs an animal and sends poison through its claws into the victim's body.

Then the centipede holds its victim and starts biting off pieces.

poison claws

mouse

Centipedes eat worms, insects, and spiders. The largest kinds sometimes eat lizards, frogs, mice, and birds.

Escaping Enemies

owl

centipede

Scorpions, shrews, and many kinds of birds and insects like to eat centipedes.

Some of these enemies look for the leggy creatures when they come out at night to hunt.

Others try to find the centipedes in their daytime hiding places.

scorpion

centipede

Usually, the centipedes use their many legs to try to run away quickly.

When they cannot escape, they use their poison claws to defend themselves—giving the enemy a painful bite!

ants

centipede

shrew

centipede

Some centipedes
defend themselves with the
help of a liquid they store
in their bodies. The liquid
makes them smell and taste
so bad that enemies don't
want to eat them.

17

Lots of Eggs

Female centipedes lay lots of little eggs.

When the baby centipedes hatch, they look very different from adults.

They are much smaller and much lighter in color.

Most kinds also start out with fewer pairs of legs.

Some female centipedes stay with their eggs to keep them safe from hungry enemies. Others bury them under a bit of soil to keep them hidden until they hatch.

eggs

young centipede

All Grown Up

As young centipedes get bigger, they outgrow their exoskeletons.

So the centipedes molt—shedding their old coverings and forming new ones that are bigger and darker.

With each molt, another important change takes place.

The centipedes grow new segments and new pairs of legs.

After many molts, they are fully grown.

The little creatures have all their legs and are ready to begin their adult lives.

new exoskeleton

old exoskeleton

Some kinds of centipedes already have all their segments and legs when they hatch. They simply grow bigger and darker with each molt.

A World of Invertebrates

An animal that has a skeleton with a **backbone** inside its body is a *vertebrate* (VUR-tuh-brit). Mammals, birds, fish, reptiles, and amphibians are all vertebrates.

An animal that does not have a skeleton with a backbone inside its body is an *invertebrate* (in-VUR-tuh-brit). More than 95 percent of all kinds of animals on Earth are invertebrates.

Some invertebrates, such as insects and spiders, have hard skeletons—called exoskeletons—on the outside of their bodies. Other invertebrates, such as worms and jellyfish, have soft, squishy bodies with no exoskeletons to protect them.

Here are four animals that are related to centipedes. Like centipedes, they are all invertebrates.

Pill Millipede

Flat-Backed Millipede

Symphylan

Pauropod

Glossary

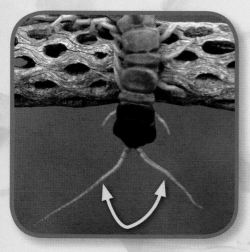

antennas
(an-TEN-uhz)
the body parts
on a centipede's
head used for
feeling and
smelling

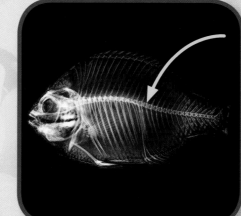

backbone
(BAK-*bohn*)
a group of
connected bones
that run along
the backs of some
animals, such as
dogs, cats, and fish;
also called a spine

segments
(SEG-muhnts)
strip-shaped
parts of a
centipede's
trunk

trunk
(TRUNGK)
the part of
a centipede's
body behind
the head

Index

Read More

Hall, Margaret.
Centipedes. Mankato, MN: Capstone Press (2006).

Merrick, Patrick.
Centipedes. Chanhassen, MN: The Child's World (2003).

Povey, Karen.
Centipede. San Diego, CA: KidHaven Press (2004).

Learn More Online

To learn more about centipedes, visit
www.bearportpublishing.com/NoBackbone–CreepyCrawlers

About the Author

Natalie Lunis has written many science and nature books for children. She lives in the Hudson River Valley, just north of New York City.